...resents

The Louisiana Purchase:

A History Just for Kids

KidCaps is An Imprint of BookCaps™
www.bookcaps.com

Table of Contents

About KidCaps

KidCaps is an imprint of BookCaps™ that is just for kids! Each month BookCaps will be releasing several books in this exciting imprint. Visit are website or like us on Facebook to see more!

Introduction

The day was July 31, 1803. Birds chirped outside of Thomas Jefferson's window in the Presidential office. From his vantage point, Jefferson could see the busy city of Washington D.C. wake up and start its day. Horse-drawn carriages carried supplies to shops, well dressed men and woman went about their business; some were buying, some were selling, others were hurrying to their offices, where they would work hard all day, doing business for the government. Some stray dogs fought in the street over some scrap of food that they had found. Jefferson took a deep breath.

As President of the United States, Thomas Jefferson felt a lot of responsibility on his shoulders. It was his job to lead this young nation through the growing pains that naturally came with being an independent country. Only thirty years ago, he remembered being a much younger man, and using a small writing table to pen the Declaration of Independence from Great Britain. Together with four other men, known as the "Committee of Five" he had spent long hours telling the British government why the Americans could no longer tolerate living under their control. Jefferson truly believed that America was destined to be the greatest nation on the face of the Earth, a great experiment in democracy for the whole world to see.

However, on this day, Thomas Jefferson was worried.

In his mind, he kept repeating one word: *tyranny*. Do you know what that word means? "Tyranny" is where one person (or a small group of people) rules over a whole country. However, instead of using their power to help the people, they use their power only to help themselves. In fact, they treat the people harshly, take advantage of them, and even hurt them. With his own eyes, Jefferson had seen the terrible effects of tyranny.

Thomas Jefferson, when he was younger, had lived in the United States under British rule. He felt that Great

Britain had made the Americans live under tyranny. The British had charged lots of money to send supplies to the colonies, they had not given them rights to vote, and they mistreated the colonists, even killing them sometimes. Now that he was the American President, elected by the people to lead the United States, Thomas Jefferson wanted to be sure that he never became a tyrant like the British had been. He never wanted to do the bad things that they had done.

The best way to make sure that the President never became a tyrant was for him to strictly obey the laws of the United States Constitution. Do you know what the Constitution is? After the colonies decided that they wanted to be independent of British rule, they decided to make a list of laws to govern their new country. Instead of giving one man all of the power (like a king or emperor) the constitution included a system of "checks and balances". It made sure that there would be a limit to what a President could do. That way, he would never become a tyrant (a bad ruler).

So, before Thomas Jefferson could make an important decision, he had to have the approval of Congress (made up of elected representatives from each state). Congress would make sure that the President never did anything to hurt the American people. At the same time, Congress could not make a new law if the President did not approve it. In that way, the writers of the Constitution made sure that the United States would never again suffer under tyranny.

President Thomas Jefferson was one of the biggest supporters of limiting the President's power. He had seen how too much power in the hands of one man tended to corrupt him, to make him go bad. But today, on this lovely summer morning, Thomas Jefferson was doing something that violated his own beliefs. He was making an important decision, and spending a lot of American money, all without the approval of Congress. He had approved a large purchase of land from France, and was hoping that he had done the right thing. But Congress had not approved the purchase, because there had not been time to tell them. Jefferson had been worried that the French would change their minds. Not, he hoped that Congress would ratify (approve) his decision. But Jefferson wondered: had he gone too far? Had he taken the first step to becoming a tyrant? Only time would tell.

This is the story of the Louisiana Purchase. Have you ever heard about this famous agreement signed between France and the United States in 1803? Do you know who was involved, how much money was exchanged, and why it was so important at the time? Do you know why we should be interested in this agreement today, over two hundred years later?

The Louisiana Purchase was signed by representatives of President Thomas Jefferson of the United States and of Napoleon Bonaparte I of France on April 30, 1803. For a cash payment of $11,250,000 (and an additional cancellation of debt amounting to $3,750,000) the United States government received a HUGE piece of land from the French (measuring about 827,000 square miles). The piece of land started at New Orleans in the south and went up the Mississippi River all the way to the Canadian border, going west as far as the Rocky Mountains.

But did you know that the Americans never expected to buy so much land? As we will see, the French actually surprised them with the generous offer of such a large territory.

Why was the Louisiana Purchase so important at the time? We will see some of the reasons in the next few sections. However, this purchase wasn't just a normal piece of business. There had been the possibility of war if a problem with New Orleans (located in the Louisiana Territory) wasn't resolved. When the representatives went from the United States to France, they knew that if they didn't find a way to make an agreement with the French, there would soon be the smell of gun smoke and cannon fire in the United States. People would die, and it would be awful.

What's more, this would be one of the first opportunities for a President to see how much power the constitution really gave him. Remember, everyone back then was scared of living under another tyranny

(like they be forced to do with Great Britain) so President Thomas Jefferson had to be careful. If he chose wrong, he could set a bad example for later presidents, who might misuse their power. He himself could even be removed from office for not following the constitution.

The story of the Louisiana Purchase is a story of young America. Taking place about thirty years after the Revolutionary War had been fought, it was a time when Americans were trying to decide what their future would be, and how they wanted their country to operate. They still had lots of enemies surrounding them, and the threat of war was everywhere. These early Americans had to find ways to keep expanding their territory and to keep supporting their fellow U.S. citizens, no matter where they lived. They had to establish diplomatic relations with foreign nations and had to know how to negotiate peace agreements. The Louisiana Purchase is one of the first success stories of a young American government, and there is a lot that we can learn from it.

Chapter 1: What Led Up To the Louisiana Purchase?

Before we can really talk more in depth about what happened during the Louisiana Purchase, and what some of its effects were, we have to know a little bit more about the background of this impressive territory. For example, how did this part of the New World come to be under French control? Did anyone else ever have any power over it? Why did the United States wait so long before taking action to acquire this land? Let's find out.

First, how did this part of the New World come to be under French control? Do you remember a little bit about the first explorers to the New World? Well, they came from all sorts of countries. Christopher Columbus was Italian, but he was sent out by the Spanish King and Queen in order to find new ways of bringing in lots of money to Spain. When he arrived in the New World in 1492, Columbus and his men explored lots of islands, including the Antilles, Hispaniola, and Cuba. He made several other expeditions in the following years, making Spain one of the first nations to really see what the New World was all about.

A little later, in 1537, a group was sent out from Spain that included a man named Álvar Núñez

Cabeza de Vaca. This group was among the first that was able to explore the area now known as New Orleans. However, why didn't the Spanish claim New Orleans for themselves? Álvar Núñez Cabeza de Vaca and the other men that were with him got caught in the middle of a powerful storm, and all but four were dead within a short time. So even if Spain had wanted to claim the area, there were no men to do it.

It was the French who finally made New Orleans their permanent home. The French had already established their territory in Quebec (back in 1608). Sometime later, they decided to explore further south. After first navigating the Great Lakes region, a French explorer named René-Robert Cavelier found the source of the Mississippi River up north. Hopping in his boat in 1682, the French explorer decided to just follow the river south, as far as he could, to see where it would lead. To his surprise, the river just kept going and going, eventually taking him to the southern part of the United States, the Gulf of Mexico.

Once the French had sailed all the way down to the Gulf, they began to return northward, setting up trading posts all along the banks of the Mississippi River. They traded furs and other goods with Native American tribes, and made a lot of money doing it. Eventually, New Orleans became a larger and more established French city, with permanent residents living there and building homes, shops, and even growing crops in the nearby fields. The city remained under French control until the outbreak of the Seven

Years' War (also called the French and Indian War) in 1754.

The French and the British had both been interested in colonizing the New World. However, as you might imagine, sometimes they stepped on each other's toes. There were several arguments about the borders of each nation's territory, and their arguments finally ended up turning into a war in May of 1754. British colonists (led by George Washington) attacked French troops. The Native Americans and the Spanish, who both saw an opportunity to get rid of the British, decided to support the French. Although things went well for the French at first, things started to get worse and worse for them. No new troops arrived to help them, and they began to lose one battle after another, eventually accepting defeat by the British in 1760.

The Spanish, who had supported the French in their fight against Britain, lost Cuba to the British. They got it back later, but only after first giving the Americans the entire territory of Florida. Angry that they had lost some land because of supporting the French, the Spanish demanded that the French give them some territory in the New World to make up for the loss (after all, the Spanish felt that it was the French government's fault that the war had been lost). The French agreed to give the Spanish government control of the Louisiana Territory, including New Orleans, in a treaty signed in 1762, called the "Treaty of Fontainebleau". However, everyone, British, French, and Spanish alike, would be able to use the very important Mississippi River for business and shipping.

Now that the Spanish were in control of the city of New Orleans, a busy shipping port, how would they treat the British? Everything went very well for a time, because the British armies were very strong and not too far away, and the Spanish did not really have a large military in the New World. However, once the Americans declared their independence from Great Britain, and a treaty was signed in 1783, the Spanish became more protective of the port of New Orleans.

In fact, in 1798, the Spanish told the Americans that they were no longer allowed to use New Orleans as a port to deliver goods. Can you imagine? The Americans weren't allowed to use this busy port anymore!

As we shall see later on, this was a huge problem, because the Americans depended on this port to supply their citizens with materials and to export product to other nations. They had also begun to rely on access to the Mississippi River for trading purposes. Although the ban against the Americans using New Orleans was later lifted in 1801, things never got quite back to how they had been. Why not? Things had changed during those few years, and Spain wasn't the owner of New Orleans and Louisiana anymore.

On October 1, 1800, a secret treaty was signed between representatives of France and Spain. It was a very strange agreement, one that did a lot of good for France and not a lot of good for Spain. One important point of the treaty (which was called the "Third Treaty of San Ildefonso") was that Louisiana would go back to French control after a few very specific conditions had been met. How did this change of ownership affect everything politically in the New World?

Up until this major change, things had been pretty quiet. There had been no major wars for some time, and the Spanish were becoming weaker and weaker. No one was really scared of them anymore. For a while, the American people, including President Jefferson, thought that the Spanish would eventually just sell New Orleans to the Americans, and that they would see that it would be the best thing for them to do. Jefferson, looking back, later wrote:

> "Spain might have retained [New Orleans] quietly for years. Her pacific dispositions, her feeble state, would induce her to increase our

facilities there, so that her possession of the place would be hardly felt by us." He went on to speculate that "it would not perhaps be very long before some circumstance might arise which might make the cession of it to us the price of something of more worth to her."[1]

Spain, in other words, had not been a threat. The Americans knew that Spain was focusing more and more on South America and on the Caribbean, and that they weren't as interested in North America anymore. Even though the Americans had lost access for a time to New Orleans (and it was later given back to them) there was never any real worry of war or serious conflict with the Spanish that couldn't be resolved by just talking. However, when France (according to some historians) forced Spain to make an unwise decision and sign the Third Treaty of San Ildefonso, basically giving France control of a huge part of the New World, the Americans began to worry. They remembered very well what the French and Indian War from only forty years before had been like, and they were worried that Napoleon Bonaparte I might try to establish a worldwide empire, which would include New Orleans and the Louisiana Territory.

Now, the Americans had seen this happening, but had not taken any stronger action. Why not? Well, do you remember what we spoke about in the beginning, how Thomas Jefferson was afraid of becoming a tyrant? He felt that the Federal Government really shouldn't

[1] http://www.monticello.org/site/jefferson/louisiana-purchase

get involved unless the people *demanded* it. Up to this point, Jefferson's own philosophy (his thoughts on life) had kept him from acting. He thought that the Federal Government should only act when the people told it to. So far, the states hadn't said anything to the government about trying to buy the land or about looking for another solution.

However, Jefferson found himself in a very dangerous position. His country was about to lose access to a key port- a port that gave food to his citizens and made the country a lot of money. What's more, a new neighbor was about to move in next door. This neighbor (France) and its ruler (Napoleon Bonaparte I) had already shown themselves to be very aggressive towards other nations (like Britain and Spain) and that gave the Americans every reason to worry. How should Jefferson respond? Let's find out some of the factors that helped President Thomas Jefferson to make a decision as to what to do with the Louisiana situation.

Chapter 2: Why Did the Louisiana Purchase Happen?

As we just saw, President Jefferson and the American people saw themselves trapped in a pretty dangerous situation. They felt like they were trapped in a corner. Something had to be done and it had to be done quickly. What were some of the factors that helped President Jefferson decide that offering to purchase the territory was the best solution? In this section, we will look at the two main factors:

- **The threat of war with France**
- **The threat of disunion within the Unites States**

Let's learn more about each of them.

The threat of war with France. Back in those days, France was acting like a bully. They were pushing around other nations and trying to get everyone to do as France wanted. However, two things happened that pushed the United States into a corner, where they were forced to make a decision. First, Spanish King Charles IV (acting in favor of the future French owners of Louisiana) signed a decree in October of 1802, putting into effect the conditions of the Third Treaty of San Ildefonso, thus officially ceding Louisiana to the French. The agent of the Spanish crown who was in New Orleans then took steps to let Americans know that (yet again) they would be blocked from using the Mississippi River and the port of New Orleans. This was bad news.

The port of New Orleans was like a lifeline for the Americans who had been moving further and further West. They needed supplies from the east, and it was too difficult to carry them over the Appalachian Mountains. What's more, they needed to export the goods that they made, and they needed places to store them until ships arrived to take them away. By 1802, New Orleans had become very important to the American economy and to their future. So when the port was closed to them, it was clear that there would be a problem. America needed access to that port, and it looked like France wouldn't be giving it to them without a fight.

In a letter written about this time, President Jefferson said:

> "This little event, of France's possessing herself of Louisiana, is the embryo of a tornado which will burst on the countries on both sides of the Atlantic and involve in [its] effects their highest destinies."[2]

President Jefferson knew that, although this event seemed "little" to some, it would have huge effects both in America and in Europe. Adding to his fear, Napoleon Bonaparte I sent thousands of troops to the

[2] http://www.monticello.org/site/jefferson/louisiana-purchase

New World, under the command of General Charles Leclerc, to stop the slave rebellion in Saint-Domingue (present day Haiti). Having so many soldiers nearby made everyone nervous. It looked like Napoleon I, having won so many military victories in Europe, was planning to establish another part of his empire in the New World. The American people could not allow a threat like that to move in next door.

The threat of disunion within the United States. As many American citizens, especially those living west of the Appalachian Mountains and who were directly affected by the actions and decisions of Napoleon I, saw what was going on, they began to get very worried. Why? Remember that in those days, slavery was still allowed in the United States, but it had been outlawed in France in 1794 (after the French Revolution). As a result, American slaveholders were afraid that the French would arrive and free all of the slaves that were living in New Orleans and Louisiana. If that happened, other slaves might revolt throughout the Unites States and try to get their freedom also. In fact, not too long after the secret treaty of 1800, Napoleon I found himself fighting the largest slave revolt in history. This revolt (in present day Haiti) would be the first one to prove successful.

The Federalist political party in the United States, who were sworn enemies of the Democratic-Republican President Jefferson, felt that Jefferson wasn't doing enough to help slaveholding Americans west of the Appalachian Mountains. They began to suggest that the states closer to Louisiana (like

Kentucky and Tennessee) secede from the national government and declare war on France. Can you imagine? Only about thirty years after the United States was formed, there were already people talking about a Civil War!

When Thomas Jefferson saw how Napoleon I was moving so many troops into the area, and he saw how many of his fellow Americans were getting worried and angry, he knew that he had to decide what to do. One option would be to simply make an offer to Napoleon I and to try and buy the land from him. Of course, Jefferson would have to hope that Napoleon I agreed, but that is something we will talk about in a moment. Jefferson wasn't only worried about Napoleon I, however; he was still very worried about breaking the law and becoming a tyrant.

As we mentioned, Jefferson was not a member of the Federalist political party that we saw earlier. He was their political enemy. Who were the Federalists? They were a very important group of politicians who believed in a strong central government. They believed that the Federal government should control everything in the United States, even a national bank. People like Thomas Jefferson, however, were really worried about the power falling into the wrong hands, and about the government becoming a tyranny. To make sure that didn't happen, they felt that the power should stay in the state governments, and that the President should only be allowed to do what the constitution tells him to.

Thomas Jefferson didn't think that the President had the authority to speak to a foreign power and to make an offer to buy land from him. However, his cabinet (the people who work closely with him) told the President to look more closely at Article 1, Section 8, and Clause 18 of the U.S. Constitution. It says:

> "The Congress shall have Power - To make all Laws which shall be necessary and proper for carrying into Execution the foregoing Powers, and all other Powers vested by this Constitution in the Government of the United States, or in any Department or Officer thereof."

This clause, often called the "elastic clause" or the "necessary and proper clause" gives Congress the right to approve Presidential actions if they are viewed as necessary for national security, or in order to make sure the rest of the Constitution is carried out correctly. Jefferson's cabinet convinced him that, although there was no law specifically saying that the President could go out and buy more land with U.S. taxpayer money, this clause gave the President a certain amount of discretion, or freedom to make individual decisions. In other words, Jefferson could have a little extra authority to make decisions when he really needed it.

At first, President Jefferson did not like the idea at all. In fact, he thought that it would make the American people angry to see their President make such a big decision without asking them first. However, as he thought more and more about the potential dangers of

France owning so much land nearby and of losing access to New Orleans forever, Jefferson finally decided to go ahead and send representatives to speak with Napoleon I. Jefferson later said about the sale:

> "It is the case of a guardian, investing the money of his ward in purchasing an important adjacent territory; and saying to him when of age, I did this for your good."

Did you understand what Jefferson was trying to say? He uses the word "ward" which is like someone you take care of. He was saying that, as President, he felt a special responsibility to the American people and to the money they had given to the government. He felt like he had made the right decision, but that many people might not have understood it until much later, like a child who needed to grow a little more before he could understand certain things about the adult world.

Now that we understand what motivated President Jefferson to finally try and negotiate the purchase of Louisiana, let's see what actually happened during the purchase itself.

Chapter 3: What Happened During the Louisiana Purchase?

When President Jefferson finally decided to try to purchase the city of New Orleans from the French, he knew that he had to send some people that he really could trust to do the job. Who did he send? The first was a man named Robert R. Livingston. Livingston was one of the men who had worked with Jefferson (on the "Committee of Five") to prepare the Declaration of Independence. He was appointed U.S. Minister to France in 1801. In January of 1803, soon after Louisiana was officially ceded to the French by the Spanish, James Monroe, a close personal friend of the President, was also sent to France. He would join Livingston in Paris in order to help negotiate the purchase of New Orleans and the surrounding area.

In a letter sent to Monroe, President Jefferson explained how important his mission was:

> "All eyes, all hopes, are now fixed on you; and were you to decline, the chagrin would be universal, and would shake under your feet the high ground on which you stand with the public. Indeed I know nothing which would produce such a shock, for on the event of this mission [depend] the future destinies of this republic. If we cannot by a purchase of the

country insure to ourselves a course of perpetual peace and friendship with all nations, then as war cannot be distant, it behooves us immediately to be preparing for that course, without, however, hastening it, and it may be necessary (on your failure on the continent) to cross the channel."[3]

According to President Jefferson, the future of the republic (the United States) was at stake. If Monroe was not successful, then there would be war. If he could not be successful in France, he should "cross the channel" to London in order to seek help there, and to get ready for war with France.

Back at home in the United States, Jefferson still had to try to convince the people west of the Appalachian Mountains not to secede and to start a war themselves. He wanted them to know that, as President, he was very interested in resolving the problems they were facing and that he was working very hard. To the governor of Kentucky, James Garrard, he wrote on January 18, 1803:

"In order, however, to provide against the hazard which beset our interests & peace in that quarter, I have determined with the approbation of the Senate, to send James Monroe, late governor of Virginia, with full powers to him and our ministers in France and Spain to enter with those governments into such arrangements as may effectually secure

[3] http://www.let.rug.nl/usa/P/tj3/writings/brf/jefl149.htm

our rights & interest in the Mississippi, and in the country eastward of that. He is now here and will depart immediately. In the meantime knowing how important it is that the obstructions shall be removed in time for the produce which will begin to descend the river in February, the Spanish minister, has, at our request, reiterated his interposition with the intendant of New Orleans."[4]

He told the governor about the trip of Monroe, and about his continued efforts to reopen New Orleans. Do you think that the governor took him seriously? Do you think that it made him feel better to know that the President was listening to his concerns? We can imagine that letters like these helped to keep the peace during those troubled times.

Do you see how hard Jefferson was trying to keep young America together? He had to worry about threats both from the outside and from the inside. It was not an easy job to do. He was depending completely on the successful negotiations between the representatives of the American and French governments. But would Livingston and Monroe have success in their mission?

When Monroe arrived on April 12, Livingston had some shocking news for him: the French wanted to sell the *entire* Louisiana Territory to the Americans, not just New Orleans! This was something that was

[4] http://memory.loc.gov/cgi-bin/query/r?ammem/mtj:@field(DOCID+@lit(tj090198))

entirely unexpected. If you remember, the Americans were really only worried about getting access to New Orleans and to the rest of the Mississippi River. But here the French had offered them over 827,000 square miles, so much land that it would nearly *double* the previous size of the United States. Why the change of heart?

Napoleon I had wanted to build a worldwide empire. He wanted not only to be strong in Europe, but also to be strong in the New World. However, he had two big problems: Saint-Domingue (present day Haiti) and Great Britain.

After coming to power, Napoleon I decided to focus his energies on Saint-Domingue, a French colony on the island of Hispaniola that was having a large problem with slave uprisings (Napoleon had reinstituted slavery in French colonies shortly before). After sending about twenty thousand troops to take back control of the island (which had always made

France a lot of money producing sugar and rum) Napoleon I was upset to see that all of his troops were dying, and that the battle was being lost. The slaves were not only fighting very well, but there were also a lot of diseases (like Yellow Fever) that were just destroying his French armies. After several years of fighting, when there were only about 7,000 French soldiers left alive, Napoleon I told them to just leave the island and go home. The French had lost, and the slaves of Saint-Domingue had won their rebellion.

What's more, France's problems with Great Britain just kept getting worse and worse. By the time the year 1803 had begun, France was preparing for war with its neighbor. Napoleon I realized that there was no point in sending any more money or men to the New World. It would be better to prepare for war in Europe and to protect his empire there. In order to do that, though, he needed money. The perfect idea came to Napoleon I: get rid of one problem (Louisiana) and solve another (lack of money) by selling the entire Louisiana territory to the Americans.

Livingston and Monroe had been authorized by the President to spend up to $10 million to buy the city of New Orleans and permission of passage up the Mississippi River. However, the French offered to sell the whole Louisiana Territory for only $15 million. In other words, for a little more money, the Americans could own, not just New Orleans, but much much more. What did Monroe and Livingston do?

Although they weren't authorized to spend so much money, they were sure that the American Government would approve it. This was the answer to all of their problems! Not only would they avoid war with France, they would get new territories for trading and exploring, and they would guarantee free access to the Mississippi River forever! After signing the agreement, Livingston said:

> "We have lived long, but this is the noblest work of our whole lives. . . From this day the United States take their place among the powers of the first rank. . ."[5]

Yes, it was a very special moment. As part of the price, France specifically asked for a cash payment of $11,250,000 and for an additional debt cancellation amounting to $3,750,000. The men got the money on loan from Great Britain and signed the agreement on April 30, 1803. The official announcement was made in the United States on July 4, just in time for the celebration Independence Day and America's birth as a nation.

The French were happy to get rid of land that they didn't want anymore and to get some much needed money for their military; the Americans were happy to have their importing/exporting problems solved and to remove the threat of war. Even Great Britain was happy because they got to do a little business-they loaned the Americans some money with interest. However, there was one country that was very unhappy with the whole arrangement. Do you know who it was? It was Spain. Why was Spain unhappy with the agreement?

When France and Spain had traded Louisiana back and forth, it was never really specified how big the territory itself really was. Also, France had promised that they would never sell Louisiana to a third party. When measuring the land later, Spain felt that it should be smaller, but the Americans felt that it should be larger. Spain also felt that France didn't really have a right to sell it, as it still belonged to Spain in a lot of ways. However, because they had no

[5] http://www.lpb.org/education/tah/lapurchase/quotes.cfm

military force to fight the decision, Spain had to accept the agreement and try to negotiate later with the Americans. Although they were unhappy, they had no choice but to accept and approve the agreement.

The Louisiana Purchase had been made.

Chapter 4: What Was It Like to be a Kid During the Louisiana Purchase?

Being a kid, it is not always easy to understand the things that adults talk about or are worried about. During the Louisiana Purchase, there were no wars, no deaths, or anything big like that. What did happen was that people were worried, and they talked a lot about it.

We mentioned in the introduction that the Louisiana Purchase was a test of young America. But more than that, it was also a test of young Americans. Think about it. Only thirty years before, these people had been fighting to establish a new nation, one that wouldn't be ruled by kings who took advantage of the people and who asked their subjects for a lot of money. Later on, these soldiers who had fought in the Revolutionary War became fathers, and they were the ones living during the time of the Louisiana Purchase.

Can you imagine being a kid back then? Imagine you lived close to the city of New Orleans. Let's say that your family had a farm, where you raised cows and pigs. The cows gave milk, which you and your family would make into butter and cheese. You would help slaughter the pigs to get pork and bacon. Then, you would sell the meat, cheese, and butter to ships in New Orleans. You could use the money to buy other things your family needed, like material for clothes, tools, wagons, horses, and so on. Would you like to have lived on a farm and worked hard every day? It would have been a very satisfying life.

Now, imagine that you hear that Americans can no longer use the port of New Orleans. How would you and your family get the things you need, and how would you sell the things your farm produced? If the port of New Orleans is closed, then you will have some real problems. You also won't be able to get any news from the east, because very few people come travelling over the mountains. What's more, you are trapped! You can't ever leave because the Mississippi River is the only way out, north or south, and now they say you can take a boat on it anymore! How would you have felt?

The, imagine that you overhear your parents talking one night about the French. Maybe your parents have heard about the terrible wars in Europe, and now the French are going to be sending their soldiers to where you live! Would you be afraid that the French would take away your farm and your animals just because you are American? A lot of people were very afraid back then. Some of them even began to talk about rebelling against President Jefferson. Do you think that would have been the right thing to do?

These weren't easy questions for anyone to answer. It would not have been easy to be a kid back then, because you would have been very worried about

what was going to happen, and whether or not there
would be a war.

Chapter 5: How Did It End?

After Livingston and Monroe had signed the agreement, it still wasn't one hundred percent official yet; Congress had to ratify (approve) it. Would they? Remember, President Jefferson didn't really have permission to buy land like that, but he felt that he was justified in doing so because of the "necessary and proper clause" of the Constitution. Although there were quite a few angry people when the announcement was made, Congress finally ratified the agreement on October 20, 1803. On November 30, Spain officially gave France all control of Louisiana, and the French held a ceremony of their own on December 20, at a building called "The Cabildo" in New Orleans.

For some time, it had looked as if a crisis had been about to sweep across the United States, and that there would be a war with France over New Orleans and the Louisiana Territory. Then suddenly, in an unexpected solution, the Americans ended up simply buying the land, and not a drop of blood was shed. The crisis had been averted, and everyone (except Spain) was happy.

While not everyone in America was completely satisfied with how Jefferson had handled the problem, everyone agreed that the new land was a good thing for the United States. With so much territory, there would be more opportunities to explore, more Native Americans to trade with, and a greater opportunity of fulfilling what many referred to as America's "manifest destiny". Have you heard that term before?

Do you remember what it means? Manifest destiny is the belief that many early Americans had about the future of the United States. They believed that the United States was destined to cover the whole North American continent, from east to west. With this large purchase of land, it looked like that dream might soon become a reality.

Jefferson would later realize that this was perhaps the most important achievement of his presidency. Although he was not happy about using the "necessary and proper clause" in the way that he had, he was convinced that he had not broken the law. Although many of his political rivals accused him of going too far by secretly approving the Louisiana Purchase, no one suggested that he be removed from the office of President or be charged with any crimes.

The French soon abandoned Louisiana for the last time, and the Spanish eventually signed an agreement with the Americans, called the Adams–Onís Treaty of 1819, which officially defined the boundaries of the Louisiana Purchase.

Chapter 6: What Happened After the Louisiana Purchase?

As we saw before, some (including Spain) complained at first that the whole transaction was illegal. They say that France was never really in complete control of the Louisiana Territory, and that according to the treaty signed with Spain, it had no right to sell any portion of the land to a third party. Is that true? If so, what would it mean? Note what one historian said:

> "The sale of Louisiana to the United States was trebly invalid; if it were French property, Bonaparte could not constitutionally alienate it without the consent of the Chambers; if it were Spanish property, he could not alienate it at all; if Spain had a right of reclamation, his sale was worthless."[6]

To be honest, France did in fact violate its treaty with Spain, which made the sale illegal. The President knew this, but did not worry too much, knowing that Spain would have no choice but to approve the agreement once it was finalized. And that is exactly what happened.

---

[6]

http://en.wikipedia.org/wiki/Louisiana_Purchase#Asserting_U.S._possession

After the Louisiana Purchase, the Unites States government had to struggle a bit to get complete control over the new territory. Because of heavy British presence that had been in the area for so long, and because of some Native American tribes who did not appreciate the Americans moving onto their lands, the Americans felt it necessary to build two military forts to protect themselves, one called Fort Osage along the Missouri River (in western present-day Missouri) and the other named Fort Madison along the Upper Mississippi River (in eastern present-day Iowa). These forts would be useful later on during the War of 1812, when the British and the Native Americans joined forces to fight against the Americans. Several more forts were built to protect New Orleans and the coast itself.

This large territory would eventually be divided up to include parts of 15 states. The first of them to be admitted to the Union was the state of Louisiana on April 30, 1812; which was exactly nine years to the day after the Louisiana Purchase had been signed. This large territory, however, went unexplored for a long time. Except for a few traders and fur trappers, no one really knew what was in those hills, and in the Rocky Mountains. Thomas Jefferson got Congress to approve a special group to be sent out, called the Corps of Discovery. About one year after the Louisiana Purchase agreement was signed, Meriwether Lewis and William Clark set out with a group of about 33 men to explore parts of the new territory along the Missouri River and to cross the

Rocky Mountains to the Pacific Ocean. Their journey was very important to the history of the United States.

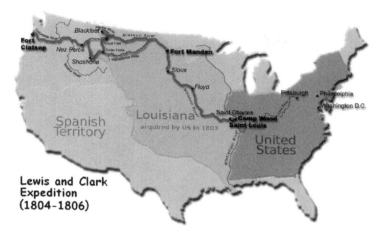

Lewis and Clark
Expedition
(1804-1806)

If it hadn't of been for the Louisiana Purchase, it would have been very difficult for Lewis and Clark to have made their journey. After all, they would have been trespassers on a foreign land. After the sale, however, they were able to explore the territory freely without worrying about British, French, or Spanish soldiers attacking them.

As the United States pushed further and further west, they eventually established what came to be called the Oregon Trail, which travelled north and west through the territory obtained from the Louisiana Purchase. As they reached the Pacific Coast, settlers soon discovered gold, and the Gold Rush began. All of these important moments in American history were made possible by the Louisiana Purchase.

However, do you remember why President Jefferson finally decided to try and purchase New Orleans from the French, even though he didn't really think that he had the authority to do so? It was because of the "necessary and proper clause" of the U.S. Constitution. Although he had previously argued that this clause should not be used to give the government or the President special powers, that is exactly what Jefferson used it for. What's more, he would not be the last.

In fact, many U.S. presidents since then have used that same clause to justify all sorts of expansions of their powers. From making sure that states don't separate whites and African-Americans to encouraging economic growth as part of Franklin Delano Roosevelt's "New Deal", the "necessary and proper clause" that Jefferson used has become an excuse to do all sorts of things. Jefferson was worried that the Federal government would get more and more power as time went by, and that is exactly what happened.

Does that mean that Jefferson was a bad guy? Not at all. What it means is that Jefferson violated his own conscience, his own philosophy on life. He had a tough decision to make, and he did the best he could, but he knew that there would be consequences. He was right.

Conclusion

The Louisiana Purchase was a test of young America. When they had their first problem with another nation, would they run, or would they stand their ground and be ready to fight? When there were problems from within its borders, would the President be like a tyrant and force the people to respect him, or would he listen to their concerns and try to resolve their problems? When there were difficult decisions to be made, would the President be quick to make the constitution fit into his own ideas, or would he try to stay within the law at all times? These were important questions. It was kind of like taking a pretty car out for a test drive- you never know how good the car really is until you get it out on the open road.

America needed an opportunity to show what she was made of, and to make sure that the world took her seriously. When the French looked like they wanted a war, American was ready to fight. However, when a peaceful solution presented itself, President Jefferson was quick to accept the solution that wouldn't involve the deaths of any American soldiers or citizens.

Do you remember the quote that Livingston said just after signing the agreement? He said:

> "We have lived long, but this is the noblest work of our whole lives. . . From this day the United States take their place among the powers of the first rank. . ."

Do you understand what he meant with that quote? In other words, he was saying that, as of that moment, the moment when America doubled its size and acquired the Louisiana Territory, the United States had become a superpower. They were officially something to be afraid of and something to be taken seriously. They had more natural resources, more friends, and more ways to make money. The future of the United States had been confirmed. The United States would become a world power.

Young America had passed its first test. Of course, there would be many more in the years to come. There would be a Civil War, World Wars I and II, and even a Cold War. Friends would become enemies, and enemies would become friends. But through it all, men like Thomas Jefferson, James Monroe, and Robert Livingston would try to sit down and figure out the best solution. Sometimes, they would be right. Sometimes, they would be wrong.

As Thomas Jefferson looked out his window that day, he had asked himself if he had gone too far. He wondered if he was becoming a tyrant, someone who is always hungry for power and who tries to dominate others and no listen to their opinions. What do you think? Did Jefferson make the right decision? Was he right to have made the Louisiana Purchase, or should he have found a different solution?

We can all learn a valuable lesson from the Louisiana Purchase. Although it wasn't an easy thing to do and although it wasn't clear if he was allowed to or not,

Jefferson tried to use his power in a way that would help others. Will you try to do the same?

Made in the USA
Columbia, SC
01 March 2019